Horned Lizard

by Dawn Bluemel Oldfield

Consultant: Darin Collins, DVM
Director, Animal Health Programs
Woodland Park Zoo
Seattle, Washington

BEARPORT PUBLISHING

New York, New York

Credits

Cover, © Matt Jeppson/Shutterstock; TOC, © Daniel Heuclin/NPL/Minden Pictures; 4–5, © Claudio Contreras/NPL/Minden Pictures; 6–7, © IrinaK/Shutterstock; 6T, © Gerrit Vyn/NPL/Minden Pictures; 7T, © Chris Mattison/FLPA/Minden Pictures; 7B, © Wayne Lynch/All Canada Photos/Alamy Stock Photo; 8, © Rolf Nussbaumer Photography/Alamy Stock Photo; 9 (T to B), © reptiles4all/Shutterstock, © fivespots/Shutterstock, and © Kruglov_Orda/Shutterstock; 10L, © Phant/Shutterstock; 10–11, © George H.H. Huey/Alamy Stock Photo; 12, © Gill Couto/Shutterstock; 13, © Jason Mintzer/Shutterstock; 14, © ebettini/iStock; 15, © Don Johnston_IH/Alamy Stock Photo; 16, © Chappell, Mark/Animals Animals; 17T, © Martin Froyda/Shutterstock; 17B, © fivespots/Shutterstock; 16–17, © BERNATSKAYA OXANA/Shutterstock and © schankz/Shutterstock; 18T, © Rolf Nussbaumer Photography/Alamy Stock Photo; 18B, © Jack Goldfarb/Design Pics Inc/Alamy Stock Photo; 19, © Mendez, Raymond/Animals Animals; 20, © John Cancalosi/Nature Picture Library; 21, © Suzanne L. Collins/Science Source; 21B, © Andrey Lobachev/Shutterstock; 22 (T to B), © ZSSD/Minden Pictures, © Satoshi Kuribayashi/Nature Production/Minden Pictures, and © fivespots/Shutterstock; 23TL, © Andrey Pavlov/Shutterstock; 23TR, © Worraket/Shutterstock; 23BL, © I WALL/Shutterstock; 23BR, © Hurst Photo/Shutterstock; Back Cover, © IrinaK/Shutterstock.

Publisher: Kenn Goin
Editor: Jessica Rudolph
Creative Director: Spencer Brinker
Design: Debrah Kaiser

Library of Congress Cataloging-in-Publication Data

Names: Bluemel Oldfield, Dawn, author.
Title: Horned lizard / by Dawn Bluemel Oldfield.
Description: New York, New York : Bearport Publishing, 2018. | Series:
   Weirder and cuter | Audience: Age 5–8. | Includes bibliographical
   references and index.
Identifiers: LCCN 2017005090 (print) | LCCN 2017009507 (ebook) | ISBN
   9781684022601 (library) | ISBN 9781684023141 (ebook)
Subjects: LCSH: Horned toads—Juvenile literature.
Classification: LCC QL666.L267 B58 2018 (print) | LCC QL666.L267 (ebook) |
   DDC 597.95—dc23
LC record available at https://lccn.loc.gov/2017005090

For more information, write to Bearport Publishing Company, Inc., 45 West 21st Street, Suite 3B, New York, New York 10010. Printed in the United States of America.

10 9 8 7 6 5 4 3 2 1

Contents

What's this weird
but cute animal?

It's a
horned lizard.

Pointy claws!

Spiky
horns!

Scaly
skin!

5

Horned lizards live in North America.

They are found in deserts, mountains, and grasslands.

There are 14 different kinds of horned lizards.

pygmy short-horned lizard

coast
horned lizard

greater
short-horned lizard

Horned lizards have many nicknames.

Some people call them horned toads, horny toads, or horned frogs.

However, these lizards are not toads or frogs!

snake

Horned lizards belong to a group of animals called **reptiles**. Snakes, turtles, and alligators are also reptiles.

alligator

turtle

A horned lizard has **scales** and short spikes.

There are sharp horns on its head.

It looks like a tiny dragon!

Horned lizards can grow to be 2 to 5 inches (5 to 13 cm) long—or about as long as a pen.

The best time to spot a horned lizard is during the day.

In the morning, the small reptiles sit in the sun to get warm.

Then they hunt for food.

Horned lizards bury themselves in sand to cool off during a hot day.

Horned lizards hunt for **insects**, such as ants.

They catch food with their sticky tongue!

Gulp!

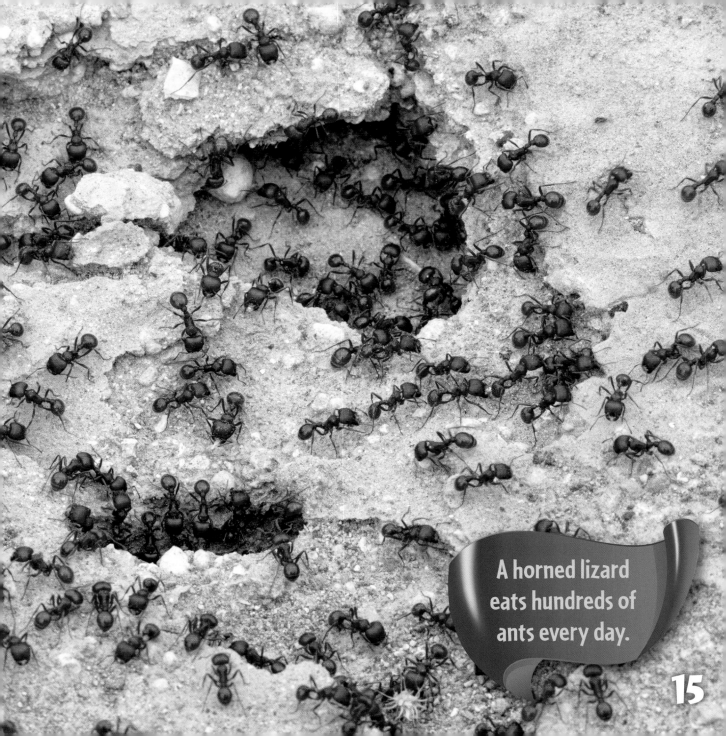

A horned lizard eats hundreds of ants every day.

Watch out!
Many animals hunt horned lizards.

roadrunner

Birds, coyotes, and snakes will attack and eat the spiky creatures.

Sometimes when a horned lizard tries to eat ants, the insects **swarm** and sting the lizard.

How do horned lizards stay safe from enemies?

Their skin blends in with sand or rocks.

This makes them hard to see.

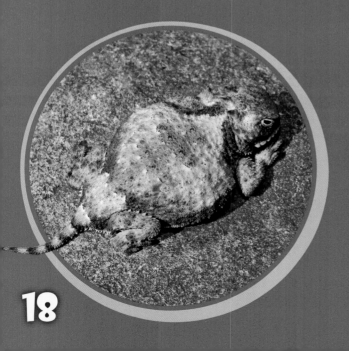

They can also puff up their bodies so they look too big to eat.

Believe it or not, some types of horned lizards can shoot blood from their eyes! This often scares away enemies.

In the summer, a female horned lizard lays eggs in a nest.

When her babies hatch, they are very tiny.

Yet, they can already hunt on their own!

a female digging a nest in the dirt

A baby horned lizard is smaller than a quarter!

More Weird Lizards

Armadillo Girdled Lizard

This lizard is covered with spiky scales. It can scare off attackers by rolling up in a ball and showing off its sharp spikes!

Draco Lizard

These reptiles use colorful flaps of skin to glide through the air. They can glide as far as 30 feet (9 m)!

Mexican Beaded Lizard

This poisonous lizard's bite is very painful and is sometimes deadly. The bites of other poisonous reptiles have no effect on this lizard.

Glossary

insects (IN-sekts) small animals that have six legs, three main body parts, two antennae, and a hard covering

reptiles (REP-tilez) cold-blooded animals that usually have dry, scaly skin, such as lizards, snakes, turtles, and alligators

scales (SKAYLZ) small pieces of hard skin that cover the bodies of some animals, including fish and reptiles

swarm (SWARM) to gather or move together in large numbers

Index

Read More

Bishop, Nic. *Lizards (Scholastic Reader Level 2).* New York: Scholastic (2014).

Marsh, Laura. *Lizards (National Geographic Kids).* Washington, DC: National Geographic Society (2012).

Learn More Online

To learn more about horned lizards, visit
www.bearportpublishing.com/WeirderandCuter

About the Author

Dawn Bluemel Oldfield is a writer who enjoys reading, traveling, and gardening. She and her husband live in Texas, where the horned lizard is the official state reptile.